DATE DUE

GROWING
VEGETABLES

Tracy Nelson Maurer

The Rourke Book Company, Inc.
Vero Beach, Florida 32964

Tracy Nelson Maurer specializes in nonfiction and business writing. Her most recently published children's books include the Bodyworks series, also from Rourke Publishing. A graduate of the University of Minnesota Journalism School, Tracy lives with her husband Mike and two children in Superior, Wisconsin.

With appreciation to gardeners Lois M. Nelson, Harvey Almstedt, and Lois I. Nelson; and to Richard J. Zondag, Jung Seed Company

PHOTO CREDITS:
All photos and illustrations © East Coast Studios except page 9 © USDA

PRODUCED & DESIGNED by East Coast Studios
eastcoaststudios.com

EDITORIAL SERVICES:
Lois M. Nelson
Pamela Schroeder

Library of Congress Cataloging-in-Publication Data

Maurer, Tracy, 1965-
    Growing vegetables / Tracy Nelson Maurer.
        p. cm. — (Green thumb guides)
    Includes bibliographical references (p.).
    Summary: Discusses the selection, planting, maintenance, and harvesting of vegetables.
    ISBN 1-55916-256-2
    1. Vegetable gardening—Juvenile literature. 2. Vegetables—Juvenile literature. [1. Vegetable gardening.
2. Vegetables. 3. Gardening.] I. Title.

SB324 .M38 2000
635'.04—dc21
                                                                00–026338

Printed in the USA

Table of Contents

Good Eating

You eat vegetables every day. (If you don't, you should!) Do you know that you're eating seeds, leaves, stems, roots, and fruits of plants? Peas are seeds. Lettuce grows as leaves. Celery comes from stems. Carrots are fat roots. Tomatoes, pumpkins, and cucumbers are really fruits of the plants.

Most gardeners believe that vegetables grown at home taste better. Fresh vegetables hold more **nutrients** (NEW tree ents), too. Try growing a small garden of your own. Plant what you like to eat.

Fun Fact

Just 20 kinds of plants, mostly corn, rice and potatoes, make up almost all of the vegetables people eat. People grow and eat more potatoes than any other plant.

You can grow vegetables from seeds or buy young plants like these peppers.

Easy Growing

Many vegetables are easy to grow. In big outdoor gardens, try planting pumpkins or cucumbers.

Vegetables also grow indoors. Lettuce, spinach, or tomatoes planted inside give you fresh vegetables even in winter.

Many vegetables grow well in outdoor gardens or in pots indoors. Where would you plant this tomato?

The soil is being washed off this rake, hoe, and shovel. Always clean your garden tools after you use them.

Before you begin planting, you need a few tools. Find a trowel, or a hand shovel, for digging. Keep a bucket or watering can to water your plants. Wear gloves to protect your hands. An outdoor gardener also needs a rake to clean and mix the soil. You need a hoe for chopping and weeding, too.

Garden Tools Care Tips

- Clean your tools after using them
- Carry your tools with the sharp ends down
- Put tools away after using them

How's Your Weather?

Gardeners must think about the weather, or **climate** (KLIH mit), where they live. A plant that grows well in Minnesota's cool summer might die in Georgia's hot summer.

A Plant Hardiness Zone Map from the U.S. Department of Agriculture shows when the last spring frost usually happens where you live. Gardeners sow, or plant, seeds after the last spring frost.

Find where you live on page 9. When should you plant seeds? Remember, colder and longer winters usually mean a shorter growing season.

Fun Fact

Some people believe the moon shows when to sow and harvest. These gardeners plant vegetable seeds under a new to full moon.

A Plant Hardiness Zone Map like the one shown here helps gardeners know what plants will grow well where they live. It also shows them when to plant in the spring.

AVERAGE DATE OF LAST FROST

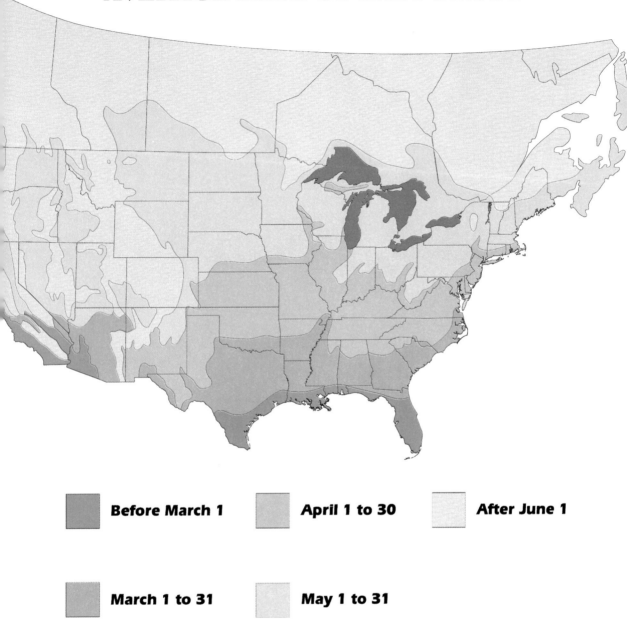

	Before March 1		April 1 to 30		After June 1

	March 1 to 31		May 1 to 31

Make a Plan

Before you plant vegetables, draw a map of your outdoor garden. Put your vegetables where the sun shines on them almost all day. Vegetable plants need plenty of room. You also want to leave space around the plants for you to weed and water.

Some plants grow well together. Gardeners call this "**companion** (kum PAN yun) planting." Tomatoes like marigolds. Stinky marigolds keep away bugs. Spinach and strawberries make good garden companions. Carrots and beans do, too.

Fun Fact

Cucumbers grow well near peas and corn, but they don't like each other. Two cucumbers planted less than 12 inches apart will try to slow each other's growth.

Marigolds planted behind this tomato help keep bugs away.

Planting Seeds

Vegetables must grow for many weeks before you can **harvest** (HAHR vist) them. Many gardeners give their vegetables a head start by planting seeds indoors before the last spring frost.

You can sprinkle small seeds into the soil. You may need to "thin" or pull out the weak seedlings later. This gives the strong seedlings room to grow.

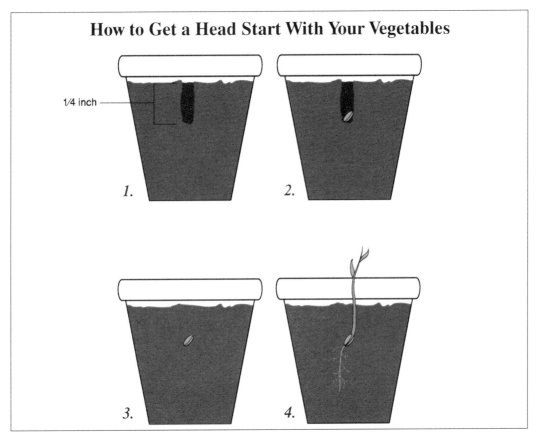

How to Get a Head Start With Your Vegetables

1/4 inch

1.

2.

3.

4.

1. Make a hole. 2. Drop in one seed. 3. Fill the hole, pat it, and water it. 4. If you cover the cup with plastic, take off the plastic when the seedling has leaves.

To start your vegetables early, put potting soil in small cups. Follow the steps on the seed packet. Usually, you need to make a hole in the soil at least 1/4" deep. Drop in one seed, fill the hole with soil, and pat it gently. Soak the soil with water and cover the cup with plastic wrap.

Dirty Work

Dirt, or soil, feeds your plants. Healthy soil makes healthy plants. Use soil from a store for your indoor plants. If you use outdoor soil, you could bring bugs into your home!

Check your outdoor soil before planting. Clean out old roots, leaves, and stones. Squeeze a handful of soil. Plants grow best in loam, a brown soil that sticks together. Loam also crumbles if you poke it.

Red clay or light brown sand makes poor gardening soil. You may need to add **organic matter** (or GAN ick MAT ur) and **fertilizer** (FUR tuh LIE zur) to your soil.

Fun Fact

Native Americans fertilized their gardens with dead fish. Some gardeners today use a "tea" made from a herring-like fish for fertilizer.

This is loam, a healthy soil. Rake well-rotted leaves or old cow droppings into your garden soil for strong plants.

Water and Weed

Most outdoor gardens need about an inch of water a week. Indoor plants may need water every day. Soak the soil under the plants. Try not to pour water on the leaves.

Weed your garden, too. "Crops" are the good plants to eat. "Weeds" are the rest. Pull out the weeds—roots and all.

Mulch helps to keep the soil moist and stop weeds. Pine straw, cocoa bean shells, or small bits of wood make good mulch. When your plants stand about four inches tall, put two inches of mulch under them.

Greedy Weeds

Weeds are greedy. They steal water and food from your plants. They hog the soil. Pull weeds out as soon as you see them.

Be sure to pull out all of the weed's roots. Shake the soil off the roots to fill in the root hole.

Happy Harvesting!

Vegetable gardeners enjoy harvesting their crops. They often share with friends, neighbors, and those in need.

Some harvesting starts early in summer. Clip the tips of lettuce and spinach during the growing season. They'll grow right back. Pick cucumbers when they look big enough. Soon you'll soon see even more cucumbers!

Harvest all of your ripe vegetables. Old vegetables left in a garden will rot and bring pests.

Gardeners often grow more vegetables than they can eat. They like to share their harvests.

Many plants need the full growing season to **ripen** (RIH pen). Often, gardeners wait until late fall before picking pumpkins and squash.

Fun Fact

Onions, carrots, potatoes, and other underground vegetables may last for months in a cool, dark place. You can freeze, pickle, or can many other vegetables. Check a cookbook to find out how.

Winter Work

A hard frost, or a night of freezing cold, kills most vegetables. Dig up old plants. Add compost, such as well-rotted grass clippings or old cow droppings, to your soil.

While the ground rests in winter, gardeners stay busy. Keep a journal. Write down which plants grew well and which did not. Start planning next year's garden.

Use the time in winter to learn more about gardening. Your public library, the Internet, and even seed catalogs are good places to look. Most gardeners love sharing tips and ideas, too.

Many gardeners write about their gardens. This helps them think of ideas for next year's garden!

GLOSSARY

climate (KLIH mit) — the normal weather for an area, including how hot or cold it gets and how much rain falls

companion (kum PAN yun) gardening — growing two different plants next to each other so that they help each other grow

fertilizer (FUR tuh LIE zur) — food for plants that gardeners add to the soil

harvest (HAHR vist) — to pick or gather the parts of plants you can eat or use

nutrients (NEW tree ents) — food for energy to grow

organic matter (or GAN ick MAT ur) — well-rotted pieces from anything that once was alive, such as old leaves, cow manure, or fish bones

ripen (RIH pen) — to become ripe and ready to harvest

People of all ages enjoy gardening. They like to help their plants grow, even when it's hard work.

INDEX

FURTHER READING

Find out more about gardening with these helpful books:

• Ambler, Wayne et al. *Treasury of Gardening.* Lincolnwood, Ill.: Publications International, 1994.

• Hart, Avery, and Paul Mantell. *Kids Garden!: The Anytime, Anyplace Guide To Sowing & Growing Fun.* Charlotte, Vermont: Williamson Publishing Co., 1996.

• Pohl, Kathleen. *Sunflowers.* Milwaukee: Raintree Publishers, 1997.

• *Rodale's Illustrated Encyclopedia of Gardening and Landscaping Techniques.* Edited by Barbara W. Ellis. Emmaus, Penn.: Rodale Press, 1990.

On-line resources:

Search for "kids gardening" on the World Wide Web to see many different sites.

• www.garden.org (c) National Gardening Association, 1999.

• www.farmersalmanac.com (c) Almanac Publishing Company, 2000.